Kwasi Addo

Proposed strategies (focusing on public policy) for incr
rural areas in Ghana

Kwasi Addo

Proposed strategies (focusing on public policy) for increased broadband penetration in the rural areas in Ghana

GRIN Verlag

Bibliografische Information der Deutschen Nationalbibliothek: Die Deutsche Bibliothek
verzeichnet diese Publikation in der Deutschen Nationalbibliografie; detaillierte bibliografische Daten sind im Internet über http://dnb.d-nb.de/ abrufbar.

1. Auflage 2010
Copyright © 2010 GRIN Verlag GmbH
http://www.grin.com
Druck und Bindung: Books on Demand GmbH, Norderstedt Germany
ISBN 978-3-656-07932-3

AALBORG UNIVERSITY, DENMARK

Master in Information and Communication Technology

(MICT)

PROPOSED STRATEGIES (FOCUSING ON PUBLIC POLICY) FOR INCREASED BROADBAND PENETRATION IN THE RURAL AREAS IN GHANA

•Kwasi Addo

Date Submitted: 15/03/2010

Table of Contents

Chapter One

PROBLEM FORMULATION AND INTRODUCTION

1.1 Project Objective

The objective of this project is to outline possible strategies (focusing on public policy) to increase broadband penetration in the rural areas in Ghana. Currently, broadband penetration in Africa is 0.3% and it is expected to grow to 1.3% in the next five years. More of that growth will be through mobile connections because the fixed infrastructure is just not there. It is therefore expected that more than 60% of broadband connections will be accounted for by High Speed Packet Download Access (HSPDA), Long Term Evolution (LTE) and WiMAX. [Source: Africa Review July 2009 edition Page 27].

The expected result of the proposed policy is to stimulate increased broadband penetration in the rural areas. This may be useful to government, telecom companies, ISPs, etc and the rural folks. This will help government to bridge the gap between the urban and rural areas. It will also be useful to sectors like agriculture, health, education, communication, finance, market information, commerce, and governance. The telecom companies, ISPs, etc, will benefit in terms of taking advantage to analyze, invest and make profit for the sale of broadband for internet connectivity in the rural areas. Some feasibility studies will need to justify its viability though. Concerning the rural folks, there will be improvement in their standard of living. This is because as will be seen later, broadband penetration brings about improvement in the per capita Gross Domestic Product (GDP) of the areas of implementation. Rural farmers may by the use of the internet have access to a broader market compared to the "limited market queens" who buy their products at very low prices and thus keeping them poor. Lots more other sectors of the economy will benefit from broadband penetration to the rural areas. For example, the financial sector and specifically the banks and insurance companies will now be in a better position to operate better in these areas. This is because of the increased means of communication.

1.2 Outcome

The outcome is to propose some policies for government that may stimulate increased broadband penetration in the rural areas. This result, if implemented by government is expected to increase per capita Gross Domestic Product (GDP) in the rural areas which Ghana as a country will benefit from.

1.3 Scope

The project study will focus on strategies in terms of public policy for increased broadband penetration in the rural areas in Ghana. Occasionally, references and comparisons may be made to broadband penetration in Europe, Asia, Africa or urban

areas in Ghana. The project may examine some strategies in terms of policies that may have been put in place in some of the countries in Africa, particularly for their rural areas which policy makers in Ghana may find as useful.

1.4 Introduction

It has been established that broadband penetration has a positive impact on a country's per capita Gross Domestic Product (GDP).

The impact is bigger for the developing countries than in the developed economies. "A 2009 World Bank Information and Communications for Development report has analyzed the impact of broadband on growth in 120 countries from 1980 to 2006, showing that each 10 percentage points of broadband penetration results in 1.21% increase in per capita Gross Domestic Product (GDP) growth in developed countries, and 1.38% increase in developing countries thus Broadband has more impact in developing than developed countries."
[Source: A National Broadband strategy for economic growth and development – Draft]

Broadband penetration in the developing countries is rather very low. Considering the above analysis of the World Bank, the impact will increase per capita GDP considerably assuming broadband is implemented in the rural areas of Ghana. This is because "least developed" areas benefit more from broadband penetration than "developed" areas.

Africa Review magazine edition of July 2009 puts broadband penetration in Africa at 0.3% which is negligible as far as penetration is concerned compared to the developed countries.

However, broadband penetration in the rural areas in Ghana is almost 0%.

In the light of the above, what are the barriers to broadband penetration in rural areas in Ghana? This is because for government to draw policies for increased broadband penetration, barriers to the current low penetration will have to be tackled in order to stimulate increase in penetration.

Also, what percentage of penetration do we consider appreciable, in other words what are the targets we will consider as increase in broadband penetration in rural Ghana?

Below are some reasons for low broadband penetration in the rural areas of Ghana.

a. Lack of infrastructure
b. Low level of computer literacy in the rural areas in Ghana
c. Public policy in favor of monopolistic stands
d. Pricing structure
e. Market size
f. Low Standard of living in the rural areas

The above barriers to broadband penetration may not apply to rural Ghana only, but also to urban Ghana and for that matter Africa as a whole.

The project will also focus on drivers of broadband penetration in the rural areas in Ghana.

1.5 Research Questions

This project is thus expected to answer the following questions

    a. What is public policy?
    b. What is broadband?
    c. What is the level of penetration of broadband in the rural areas in Ghana?
    d. What is meant by Strategy (in the context of public policy)?
    e. What strategies (public policies) are to be put in place to increase broadband penetration in the rural areas in Ghana?
    f. What are the benefits of broadband penetration to the rural populace in Ghana?

1.6 Methodology

    Literature Review

Considering the above, what strategies, in terms of public policy should be put in place to increase broadband penetration in the rural areas of Ghana?

Chapter Two

LITERATURE REVIEW

2.1 PUBLIC POLICY

Simply put, Public Policy is a set of rules that the public must abide by. They could be documented and enacted through law, regulation, executive order, court order, or official letter that explains the policy decided by the country's representatives or local authorities.

2.2 INTERNET ACCESS

The internet has grown to capture the entire world of information communications technology. This not withstanding, the speed to accessing information and services on the internet leaves much to be desired especially in developing countries like Ghana where bandwidth is a scarce resource. The duration of access to information and services on the internet is based on the capacity of bandwidth that is used to transmit information, the memory size and processor capacity of the transmitting and receiving devices. A bigger bandwidth means a faster data transfer rate that also means a faster performance of the internet, while a slower performance, which is a nightmare for the user, means a smaller bandwidth or lower data transfer rate Bandwidth is measured in kilobits or megabits per second (kbps/mbps) based on the data transfer rate.

2.3 DEFINITION OF BROADBAND

Broadband simply means a high data rate internet access. It enables high speed downloads and uploads of digital contents and services. There are however varying opinions in terms of the exact data rate to describe it. This is because there is no precise data rate to determine broadband. According to the Organization for Economic Cooperation and Development (OECD), data rate of 256kbps or faster in terms of download is Broadband. The US Federal Communications Commission (FCC) on the other hand describe broadband as data rate of 768kbps or faster.
http://en.wikipedia.org/wiki/Broadband_Internet_access cited 10/10/2009 @ 14:00
The underlying factor is that broadband is a high data rate internet access.

It must also be noted that broadband can be deployed on any network infrastructure such as cable networks, DSL (Digital Subscriber Line), satellite and wireless technologies. The important issue is that the infrastructure should have a high data rate internet access which falls within the capacity described in the paragraph above. The cost depends on the architecture of the infrastructure and availability of existing infrastructure, density of the customers and other environmental considerations.

In most parts of Africa, internet access is very slow as a result of extremely low data rate internet access. It stands to reason that despite using the internet, users do not have access

to broadband, based on the definitions given in the paragraph above. It is mostly dial up of 56 kbps which falls far short of the definitions given.

In broadband terms, large disparities exist between the "developed world" and "developing worlds" like Africa not only in terms of service availability, but also in terms of cost and access to technology. This therefore poses a serious challenge to policy makers and ICT engineers and professionals in Africa as to how best they can increase broadband penetration in Africa and especially in the rural areas where the bulk of the population live. This chapter will examine policies and how they influence penetration of broadband in the developed countries and that of the developing countries.

2.4 POLICY ISSUES

Governments are now aware of the importance of broadband penetration in terms of its role in improving per capita GDP. This calls for some strategies which depend on the country or group (of countries) in question and what strategies should be tailored to stimulate broadband penetration in their countries or block.

Strategy can be in several forms, examples are technology, policy, etc. As stated earlier, the project will take a look at public policy as a tool to stimulate broadband penetration in the rural areas in Ghana. The project will take a look at how policy stimulates broadband use in the Developed and Developing countries. It will also take a look at factors that influence broadband penetration in these cases.

Policies should be based on some set targets that have to be achieved. In other words, there should be some objectives or goal(s) that government should set out to do or achieve in order to increase broadband use. For example, what percentage of the population should have access to broadband within a certain period of time? What percentage of rural dwellers should have access to broadband in the next 2 years? These are issues that should be addressed by the state and with some public policy. Based on the set objectives, government can then tailor some policies to achieve the set objectives.

In the case of this project, the public policy issue is what policies should be put in place to increase broadband penetration in the rural areas of Ghana?

The subsequent writing will take a look at policies that stimulate broadband penetration in Developed and Developing countries.

2.5 BROADBAND POLICY IN DEVELOPED AND DEVELOPING COUNTRIES

Even though broadband penetration implementation in the developed and developing countries may be similar in terms of set objectives, certain factors however, influence the outcome of the set objectives resulting in different results. These factors include income levels, literacy levels, commitment to policy implementation and market behavior, etc.

influence the achievement of set targets. These are what spell out the differences between Developed and Developing countries. The remaining part of this chapter will take a look and make some analysis in both cases. The project will then look at the case of Africa which is a typical case of the developing world, then settle on Ghana and its rural broadband penetration which is the focus of this project.

2.5.1 Broadband Strategies in Developed Countries (Using OECD)

Member countries of the Organization for Economic Cooperation and Development (OECD) are examples of developed countries. These are countries with high income levels, high rate of computer literacy, constant stimulation of broadband use with content and services, and no issues with cable connectivity throughout the country. These are some of the characteristics of developed countries. As a matter of fact, most of these countries have succeeded in developing policies, content and services that stimulate broadband usage. As a result, penetration of broadband is very high in percentage terms compared to those of the developing countries that have very low percentages in broadband penetration normally less than 1%. There are very few exceptions such as Morocco, Tunisia, Egypt and some others that have fairly reasonable "high percentages" of broadband penetration. The focus of these countries is to turn out to be information society based as compared to the Agriculture based economies of the developing countries.

In broadband bandwidth terms, developed countries normally have 1Mbps and above unlike developing countries 56 kbps dial up.

These countries already have cable connectivity to almost all homes and industries. As a result, there is more broadband usage in the homes compared to those of the developing countries where basic access to telephone services is an issue. Most homes in the developing countries have no access to telephone services thus the term digital divide between the developed and developing worlds.

Another important characteristic of the developed countries is that as a result of the demand for content and services, broadband penetration is high. Most financial services, public services and other utility services are on-line and as a result, there is the demand for them. Others like games and social networking sites are easily accessible.

The developed countries normally have energy to power their systems in both the urban and rural setups. Energy is not an issue because it can be obtained anytime and anywhere without much difficulty. There are stores of backups to supply power should there be a possible blackout.

The developed countries in most cases belong to some regional or international bodies or blocks where an overall framework for broadband is drawn for member states. The individual member countries however have their own policies that fit into the overall policy framework of the organization.

2.5.2 European Union

It comprises of 27 sovereign states that have acceded to the European Union (EU).
EU members adhere to the same framework in terms of policies stimulating broadband development and penetration. There are however, some differences in how their national markets work.

The current regulatory framework aims at stimulating competition in the market for broadband services and telecom services among member states. In several member states, the incumbent operator owns telecoms and cable networks, and as a result limits facility based competition in those countries.

The EU commission has initiated a number of projects to stimulate broadband growth. These are included in the e-Europe plan 2000 – 2002 had set as its objectives as follows,
   a. cheaper, faster and more secure internet
   b. investment in people and skills
   c. greater use of the internet

Their next e-Europe plan 2005 were as follows
   a. modern online public services
   b. dynamic e- Business environment
   c. widespread broadband access
   d. secure information infrastructure

Then finally in i2010 which is a follow up to e-Europe plan 2005, the objectives are
   a. single European single space, innovation and investment in research
   b. Better public service and quality of life.

It is obvious that each stage develops on the preceding stage in terms of value and services. The e-Europe 2000-2002 was the initial stage that targeted cheaper, faster and more secure internet. It also thought of the need to educate users and make them computer literate and thus invested in people and skills. Finally, the plan also tried to stimulate a greater use of the internet. The next plan was e-Europe plan 2005 that developed upon e-Europe 2000-2002, by providing online public service and the environment to do business. It further went on to provide widespread broadband access and secured information infrastructure.

The i2010 plan seeks a single European space and also to bring innovation and investment in research. It is also to ensure a better public service and quality of life. I2010 is Innovative in the sense of bringing online new services and applications where stakeholders can sit at home and transact their businesses. These businesses can be public or private. The websites of various state and private entities are expected to play very important roles.

The national policies fit very well into the EU programs as they are expected to move in the same line of implementation.

It is obvious that developed countries belonging to various groupings have several advantages. Some of these are benefits like sharing ideas and expertise at the regional groupings level. Also some advantages of economies of scale may be enjoyed by member countries.

Chart 2.1

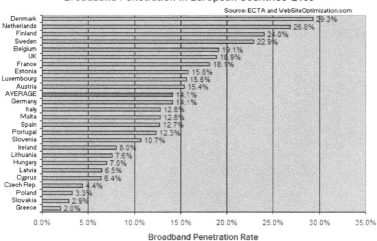

Broadband Penetration in European Countries Q106

(source: http://www.websiteoptimization.com/bw/0609/european-broadband-penetration-b.gif cited 24/02/2010 @ 09:32am) Table is Broadband penetration for 2006

2.5.3 South Korea

It should also be noted that it is not only Developed countries that are associated with high broadband penetration rate. There are some exceptional cases like South Korea that have very high penetration of broadband. According to World Bank statistics, South Korea's GDP is worth US$ 929 billion which is approximately 1.5% of the world economy. The per capita GDP is US$16,450 [source IMF Report for 2009]. Being an early mover into broadband, it has for a number of years been the leading country in terms of penetration of broadband rate. It may not be classified as a developed country and income levels may not be to the level of the developed countries. It must be noted that it is also not a developing country. In fact, it is a middle income country. Different circumstances have resulted in South Korea's ability to achieve such high broadband

11

penetration rate. As a matter of fact, South Korea is rated as one of the countries with the highest rate of broadband penetration globally. Their circumstances are different in so many ways. Their broadband bandwidth was 4Mbps in 2004 which is higher than in Europe's 2Mbps. It has probably reached its saturation level in terms of penetration of broadband rate. Virtually every corner, homes, taxis and factories have broadband connectivity. Several factors have accounted for this interesting development. These are;

a. Geography and demographics
b. Facility based competition
c. Price
d. Internet cafes (PC bang)
e. Available content
f. Government policy

It has been observed that more than 50% of households live in apartment complexes. Also, 93% of workers live 4km radius of central office. Connectivity cost is therefore low, in fact, as low as 14% the average cost of broadband connectivity globally. It is important to note that the block wirings of the apartments are owned by the landlords. The internet cafes (baangs) have stimulated the broadband services in especially the demand for on line games. Prices of broadband services measured in MB are one of the lowest one can come across in the world. Meanwhile, the Koreans are willing to pay more for higher bandwidth availability. It must be noted that the cafes provide a critical mass for the content providers. Though entertainment may be important in terms of services, educational services (complex education) are also areas that stimulate broadband use. Another admirable initiative of South Korea is that the amount paid for 3G licenses are put into research in the telecom sector and other network investments.

South Korea's progress in broadband penetration did not start now. In the 1980s, the government had already provided the country with a nationwide backbone for broadband services. There were other infrastructure developed for the public, private and others like the educational institutions.

The case of South Korea is enough to show that high penetration of broadband results from proper planning and investment in the broadband infrastructure. Others include skills development, content development and stimulating growth in the use of broadband services and urban planning. Urban planning is organized in a way that flats which are residential accommodation for workers are based quite close to the central offices. It is therefore cheaper to implement broadband in their residences and offices than in other countries where residential areas are far apart from each other and their offices. Meanwhile, the landlords arrange to get cables to the residences which enables a one touch connection to the flats and cheaper to connect.

2.5.4 Broadband Policies in Developing Countries

These are countries where universal access to basic telephone services is still an issue. As a result of this, penetration of broadband is very slow. This is because cables penetration in these countries is limited to certain urban areas with virtually nothing in the rural settings. Copper cables for transmission which are being used are not the best high bandwidth transmission for Asynchronous Digital Subscriber Lines (ADSL). The result is very slow transmission speed on the internet. Other characteristics of these countries are low income levels, high illiteracy rates, lack of ICT skills and low rates for broadband use. Another important issue is energy to power systems. Most developing countries lack energy for their generators or dams for hydro power. Under such circumstances, penetration of broadband may not be relevant. Another observation is that these countries normally do belong to some regional groupings or blocks, however the commitment to these bodies in terms of their functions is just not there. In other words, they operate independently though on document, there is some kind of grouping. However, in recent times, lots of these countries are working to increase their penetration of broadband though it is still low. This is because they find it as a way to ensure internet access and increase the general standard of living. Also, some studies have shown that developing countries benefit more from broadband penetration than the developed countries in terms of GDP growth. This has been stated in the earlier chapter, based on a World Bank study. The current mobile and wireless technology has enabled internet access from the remotest of rural areas. However, considering the fact that there is a direct relationship between income and penetration of broadband (at least to some levels of income), then the developing world has much to do. This is the result of low incomes and expensive broadband usage, internet access to a large extent is a non-starter. It is partly because of these reasons that OECD members have made gains compared to the modest by the developing world.

Whereas the developed world has between 2001 and 2005 increased from 2.9 per 100 inhabitants to 13.6, the developing world has less than 1%. It is for this reason that some argue that broadband is not relevant in the developing world. This point, to some extent is relevant in the sense that limited infrastructure does not encourage broadband penetration. However, since 2006, rapidly falling prices for broadband brought about some limited improvement of broadband penetration in the developing countries. Secondly, mobile and wireless technologies have also increased the current situation because broadband can be implemented in these media. Some government commitments to infrastructure have also increased penetration of broadband in some of these countries.

As stated above, with falling prices of broadband worldwide, the situation will make it affordable to all eventually. Broadband prices have fallen in the last two years by about 40%.

(Source of figures: From Page 672-690 Adoption of Broadband Services: The role of national policies by Morten Falch)

2.5.5 BROADBAND PENETRATION IN AFRICA

Africa is the second largest and second most populous continent in the world. With a size of 30,368,609 sq km, Africa's population is over 1 billion. Africa covers 6% of the total surface space in the world and 20.4% of the total land area. Africa accounts for 14.8% of the world population.

The continent is surrounded by the Mediterranean to the north, both the Suez Canal and the Red Sea along the Sinai Peninsula to the northeast, the India Ocean to the southeast, and the Atlantic Ocean to the west. Not counting the disputed territory of Western Sahara, there are 53 countries, including Madagascar and various island groups, associated with the continent.

http://en.wikipedia.org/wiki/Africa#Territories_and_regions cited 18/10/09 @ 4.26am

Until recently, there was only one submarine fiber-optic cable: the less efficient SAT-3 cable in Western Africa, and last updated in 2002. Those with no access to that cable are forced to use expensive and slow satellite links.

http://www.nytimes.com/2009/08/10/technology/10cable.html?_r=1 cited 18/10/09 @ 4.50am

In recent times however, a few submarine fiber-optic cables have arrived in Africa eg GLO 1 (London – Accra).

A couple of months ago, Africa Development Bank (AfDB) approved financing of a US$66 million for the MAIN ONE cable company to develop a submarine fiber optic along the West Africa coast (7,000km Lisbon – Accra, Lagos). Other investments in Africa by AfDB are EaSSy submarine cable and two satellites (Rascom and New Dawn). The total value of these projects is US$240 million.

14

Four more submarine fiber systems are expected to be added in East Africa. The Teams cable will connect Mombasa to the United Arab Emirates, while the East African Submarine Cable System will be expected later.

Despite these developments, there is lack of infrastructure to fully see the numbers grow. For example, only 5% of Africa has access to reliable electricity. Also, there are not enough gateways to the undersea cables that connect continents to the internet. It means that much of Africa still connect to satellites which are slow and expensive.

http://www.afdb.org/en/news-events/article/afdb-supports-submarine-fiber-optic-cable-for-western-africa-4710/ cited 06/12/2009 @ 21.11 GMT

While broadband penetration in the "developed world" is relatively high, in Africa, a different story is told. As late as 2002, fixed line (on which broadband can be implemented) penetration in Africa was 2.8 % compared to Europe's 41%. Africa has not been able to rely on traditional methods for fast internet access and services. This is because as stated earlier on, the infrastructure is just not there. There are old and in-efficient satellites, very few cables for broadband penetration. Considering the above statistics, it is obvious that broadband penetration in Africa is only in its infant stages with users as at 2002 numbering in thousands only compared to its huge population.

As a matter of fact, Africa is the last continent where broadband is not widely spread. In other words, broadband penetration is extremely low. The broadband penetration in Africa is barely 0.4%. Most African countries have some form of strategies to increase broadband penetration in their countries. However, broadband penetration is very low. Several reasons account for this unfortunate development. Common characteristics among these countries are lack of capital to boost broadband infrastructure, low income levels, per capita GDP is less than US$20,000, low level of education and low understanding of the use of internet. Policy makers in Africa do not appreciate and understand broadband as a tool for growth and development and also to increase GDP per capita until lately.

Some phone companies have started deploying broadband services by utilizing DSL, VSAT and occasionally cable technologies. In some cases in Africa, the incumbent is likely to wholesale broadband services to the Internet Service Providers (ISPs) who then resell to subscribers. This has generally been the trend. Currently however, this type of "monopoly" is slowly being broken with some kind of "private participation" coming into play.

2.5.6 BROADBAND PENETRATION IN GHANA

Ghana is in West Africa and shares boundaries with the following countries, Burkina Faso (North), Togo (East), Ivory Coast (West) and the Atlantic Ocean (South). Ghana has a population of 23,887,812 as at 2009 (source census bureau). As at 2008, the Gross National Income per capita was US$670.00.

Ghana covers an area of 238,528 sq km, with over a hundred different dialect, the major ones are Akan, Ewe, Ga and Moshi-Dagomba. Basically an Agricultural country that produces more raw materials, Ghana is the 2nd largest producer of cocoa in the world. Currently, she produces over 700,000 metric tones of cocoa annually. Ghana has over 60% of the workforce in the Agriculture sector. She has gold, timber and produces other food stuff though on subsistence scale. Tourism is currently being boosted and rates as the 4th largest foreign exchange earner for the country.

Ghana is generally not different from the "story of Africa" as explained in the earlier paragraphs. Ghana ranks 28 in Africa in terms of internet penetration which is only 4.2%. Broadband penetration in Ghana is 0.3%. Cable infrastructure is not wide spread and limited to the cities and some regional and district capitals.

(source: http://www.internetworldstats.com/stats1.htm cited 06/12/2009 @ 14:01:00) ???

It is obvious from the above that incomes are generally low in Ghana and not to the levels that can conveniently "push" in the internet market with GDP per capita of US$20,000 and more. Also, Ghana is basically an Agriculture based economy and not knowledge based economy.

However, with very good public policy, the country can move from its present Agriculture based economy to that of information service based economy. It all depends on how public policy is designed to achieve it.

2.5.7 BROADBAND PENETRATION IN RURAL AREAS IN GHANA

As discussed earlier, broadband penetration in Ghana is very low or negligible. In percentage terms, it is about 0.3%. It must be noted that this figure is mainly urban dominated.

On a more serious note, broadband penetration in the rural areas in Ghana is virtually approaching 0%. Implementing broadband in the rural areas is normally done by the mining companies who explore minerals and need this technology to communicate with their principals abroad, suppliers, relatives and friends. They may also need it to access some services provided by the various ISPs. This is implemented in VSAT equipment or some old inefficient satellite. This is because the cables to those rural areas are to a large extent non-existent.

There are several activities in the rural areas that may demand the need for broadband penetration. Sectors like health, agriculture, education, financial services and general internet use by the rural folks are some reasons that may justify broadband use. However, the infrastructure to enable its implementation is non existent. Furthermore, the old and inefficient satellites that may cover these areas are very expensive.

Concerning the health sector, there is virtually no application of internet services in the rural areas as at now. Clinics and health centers in the rural areas operate without any

internet access. Areas like videoconferencing that could help transfer knowledge from the "well endowed" urban hospitals to the "less endowed" rural health care centers are just not affordable.

Education is another sector that needs the services of internet services and broadband for that matter. There are several secondary schools and teacher training colleges in the rural areas that require broadband for internet access. Unfortunately, the non existence of infrastructure limits them to normally 56kps dial up technology which makes internet access very slow and boring. A few universities that are set up in the rural areas also cannot afford broadband internet access.

Most well established financial institutions do not set up in the rural areas. The best is to open an agency where a lot of paper work is done and moved to the next bigger branch in the district or region. It is mainly the rural banks that operate mostly using some kind of Local Area Network (LAN). A few of them use the normal 56kps dial up for some restricted internet access.

Though internet access and for that matter broadband implementation will be relevant to the Agriculture sector especially in the rural areas, internet access is not available and also the technical staff themselves have no basic computer training to appreciate its use. Energy to power the systems is a major issue that will be difficult to tackle especially in the rural areas. Some attempts have been made in recent times to get power to rural areas but then there is more to be done. Without abundant energy, the dream of 50% broadband penetration in the next 5 years will be a mirage.

Another huge hindrance to internet access in the rural areas is the low level of income of a large section of the populace. With a very low GDP per capita of US$670 in Ghana, the bulk of those living in these areas earn less than a dollar a day. This makes the use of the internet very expensive to users.

In the light of the above issues raised, drawing public policy (strategies) for broadband penetration in rural areas in Ghana should consider the following:

  a. Cheaper, faster and more secure internet
  b. Investment in people and skill
  c. Greater use of the internet
  d. Investment in broadband infrastructure
  e. Reduction in the cost of access devices
  f. Some tax holiday for firms that implement broadband in rural areas in Ghana
  g. Joint partnership between government and private companies to implement broadband in the rural areas in Ghana
  h. Breaking the monopoly of the incumbent
  i. Power (Energy) issues need be addressed

These issues will be thoroughly discussed in the next two chapters after the set targets for broadband penetration in the rural areas have been discussed in the next chapter.

The tables on the next pages give a vivid account of internet usage in Africa.

Chapter Three

STATISTICS AND SET TARGETS.

3.1 Statistics

This chapter will be dedicated to statistics about internet penetration in Africa, compare to the world figures and also another table to compare African countries. The project will take the draft report of Ghana Broadband Strategy and spell out the targets as set by the proposals.

The table below (Table 3a) gives a picture of internet access in Africa. It compares the total of Africa in terms of internet use to the rest of the world.

Table 3a

Internet Usage Statistics for Africa
(Africa Internet Usage and Population Stats)

INTERNET USERS AND POPULATION STATISTICS FOR AFRICA

RICA REGION	Population (2009 Est.)	Pop. % in World	Internet Users, Latest Data	Penetration (% Population)	Use Growth (2000-2009)	% Users in World
al for Africa	991,002,342	14.6 %	67,371,700	6.8 %	1,392.4 %	3.9 %
st of World	5,776,802,866	85.4 %	1,666,622,041	28.9 %	367.5 %	96.1 %
RLD TOTAL	6,767,805,208	100.0 %	1,733,993,741	25.6 %	380.3 %	100.0 %

TES: Internet Usage and Population Statistics for Africa are for September 30, 2009. Population numbers are based on res from the U.S. Census Bureau. The Internet usage numbers come mainly from data published by Nielsen Online , ITU, WW, and other trustworthy local sources. Data from this table may be cited, giving the due credit and establishing an active back to Internetworldstats.com. Copyright © 2009, Miniwatts Marketing Group. All rights reserved.

3.2 Implication of Internet Users and Population Statistics for Africa
Accounting for 14.6% of the world population means that Africa can do better in the internet penetration than the 3.9% internet users.

Internet penetration in Africa is 6.8% compared to the world average of 28.9%. This simply means that Africa falls far short in term of internet penetration. Various methods will be suggested to address these short falls in subsequent chapters of this project.

In terms of use growth, it is important to note that Africa has made almost 1,400% from year 2000 -2009.

Table 3b

INTERNET USAGE STATISTICS FOR AFRICA

AFRICA	Population (2009 Est.)	Internet Users Dec/2000	Internet Users Latest Data	Penetration (% Population)	User Growth (2000-2009)	% Users in Africa
eria	34,178,188	50,000	4,100,000	12.0 %	8,100 %	6.1 %
jola	12,799,293	30,000	550,000	4.3 %	1,733.3 %	0.8 %
jin	8,791,832	15,000	160,000	1.8 %	966.7 %	0.2 %
swana	1,990,876	15,000	120,000	6.0 %	700.0 %	0.2 %
·kina Faso	15,746,232	10,000	140,000	0.9 %	1,300.0 %	0.2 %
·undi	9,511,330	3,000	65,000	0.7 %	2,066.7 %	0.1 %
neroon	18,879,301	20,000	725,000	3.8 %	3,525.0 %	1.1 %
·e Verde	429,474	8,000	102,800	23.9 %	1,185.0 %	0.2 %
tral African Rep.	4,511,488	1,500	19,000	0.4 %	1,166.7 %	0.0 %
·d	10,329,208	1,000	130,000	1.3 %	12,900.0 %	0.2 %
noros	752,438	1,500	23,000	3.1 %	1,433.3 %	0.0 %
igo	4,012,809	500	155,000	3.9 %	30,900.0 %	0.2 %
igo, Dem. Rep.	68,692,542	500	290,000	0.4 %	57,900.0 %	0.4 %
·e d'Ivoire	20,617,068	40,000	660,000	3.2 %	1,550.0 %	1.0 %
·outi	724,622	1,400	13,000	1.8 %	828.6 %	0.0 %
·pt	78,866,635	450,000	12,568,900	15.9 %	2,693.1 %	18.7 %
iatorial Guinea	633,441	500	12,000	1.9 %	2,300.0 %	0.0 %
·rea	5,647,168	5,000	200,000	3.5 %	3,900.0 %	0.3 %
iopia	85,237,338	10,000	360,000	0.4 %	3,500.0 %	0.5 %
·on	1,514,993	15,000	90,000	5.9 %	500.0 %	0.1 %
nbia	1,778,081	4,000	114,200	6.4 %	2,755.0 %	0.2 %
ina	23,887,812	30,000	997,000	4.2 %	3,223.3 %	1.5 %
nea	10,057,975	8,000	90,000	0.9 %	1,025.0 %	0.1 %
nea-Bissau	1,533,964	1,500	37,100	2.4 %	2,373.3 %	0.1 %
iya	39,002,772	200,000	3,359,600	8.6 %	1,579.8 %	5.0 %
otho	2,130,819	4,000	73,300	3.4 %	1,732.5 %	0.1 %

eria	3,441,790	500	**20,000**	0.6 %	3,900.0 %	0.0 %
ya	6,324,357	10,000	**323,000**	5.1 %	3,130.0 %	0.5 %
dagascar	20,653,556	30,000	**316,100**	1.5 %	953.7 %	0.5 %
awi	15,028,757	15,000	**139,500**	0.9 %	830.0 %	0.2 %
i	13,443,225	18,800	**200,000**	1.5 %	963.8 %	0.3 %
uritania	3,129,486	5,000	**60,000**	1.9 %	1,100.0 %	0.1 %
uritius	1,284,264	87,000	**380,000**	29.6 %	336.8 %	0.6 %
yotte (FR)	223,765	---	---	---	---	0.0 %
rocco	31,285,174	100,000	**10,300,000**	32.9 %	10,200.0 %	15.3 %
zambique	21,669,278	30,000	**350,000**	1.6 %	1,066.7 %	0.5 %
nibia	2,108,665	30,000	**113,500**	5.4 %	278.3 %	0.2 %
er	15,306,252	5,000	**80,000**	0.5 %	1,500.0 %	0.1 %
eria	149,229,090	200,000	**11,000,000**	7.4 %	5,400.0 %	16.3 %
nion (FR)	812,813	130,000	**280,000**	34.4 %	115.4 %	0.4 %
anda	10,746,311	5,000	**300,000**	2.8 %	5,900.0 %	0.4 %
nt Helena (UK)	7,637	n/a	**1,000**	13.1 %	n/a	0.0 %
e Tome & Principe	212,679	6,500	**24,800**	11.7 %	281.5 %	0.0 %
negal	13,711,597	40,000	**1,020,000**	7.4 %	2,450.0 %	1.5 %
rchelles	87,476	6,000	**32,000**	36.6 %	433.3 %	0.0 %
rra Leone	5,132,138	5,000	**13,900**	0.3 %	178.0 %	0.0 %
nalia	9,832,017	200	**102,000**	1.0 %	50,900.0 %	0.2 %
ith Africa	49,052,489	2,400,000	**4,590,000**	9.4 %	91.3 %	6.8 %
Jan	41,087,825	30,000	**4,200,000**	10.2 %	13,900.0 %	6.2 %
aziland	1,337,186	10,000	**80,000**	6.0 %	700.0 %	0.1 %
nzania	41,048,532	115,000	**520,000**	1.3 %	352.2 %	0.8 %
to	6,031,808	100,000	**350,000**	5.8 %	250.0 %	0.5 %
nisia	10,486,339	100,000	**2,800,000**	26.7 %	2,700.0 %	4.2 %
anda	32,369,558	40,000	**2,500,000**	7.7 %	6,150.0 %	3.7 %
stern Sahara	405,210	---	---	---	---	0.0 %
nbia	11,862,740	20,000	**700,000**	5.9 %	3,400.0 %	1.0 %
nbabwe	11,392,629	50,000	**1,421,000**	12.5 %	2,742.0 %	2.1 %
TAL AFRICA	**991,002,342**	**4,514,400**	**67,371,700**	**6.8 %**	**1,392.4 %**	**100.0 %**

3.3 Set Targets

According to the draft of Ghana's Broadband Strategy, the country aims to achieve the following;

a. 50% penetration of broadband in the next 5 years from the current 0.3%.

 b. Increase broadband bandwidth from 256kbps to 2mbps within the 5 year period.

c. Broadband penetration is expected to post a growth of 6.9% over the 5 year period.

These targets can be achieved when the commitment of the government towards high broadband penetration all over the country is implemented to the letter and spirit of its commitment. Energy to power the systems is an issue that needs to be tackled in all firmness. No amount of success of broadband penetration can be achieved without energy.

Several measures may have to be taken to ensure the success of the objectives. These include a possible direct government intervention, private sector financing and collaboration between government and private sector. This is because it calls for massive investments to attain the above objectives.

The next chapter will take a deeper look at the draft document spelling out details government strategies (policies) to achieve the above targets. It will consider strategies that government wants to take to achieve these targets.

Chapter Four

GOVERNMENT PROPOSED STRATEGIES FOR BROADBAND PENETRATION IN GHANA

4.1 Summary of Government Strategies

A Draft Document titled "A National Broadband Strategy for Economic Growth and Development" has proposed the following measures to achieve increased penetration of broadband in Ghana;

a. Reduce Broadband cost by 80%

b. Reduce Customer Premise Equipment (CPE) and PCs by 90%

c. 50% broadband penetration by 2015

According to the draft document, with the above measures, the following will be achieved within a 5 year period. These are

- a.   50% broadband penetration
- b.   GDP growth of 6.9% in 5 years
- c.   Increase broadband bandwidth from 256kps to 2mbps from 2010 to 2015

Other benefits identified by this project that can be achieved are
- a   Cheaper and more convenient way to communicate compared to other media
- b   Gradual move from the Agriculture based economy to knowledge based economy
- c   Cut down on unnecessary travels at a high cost
- d   Bring the world to the door step of the rural folks
- e   Businesses (including those in the rural areas) will boom
- f   Broadband offers a better and larger platform for marketing, advertising, education, health, finance, banking, insurance, governance, etc.

This project will analyze the draft report even though it is yet to get government approval, because it is the only major document available in terms of government paper on penetration of broadband in Ghana.

With the above measures in place by 2015, the economy is expected to increase GDP growth by 6.9% in the next 5 years, while at the same time broadband penetration is expected to increase by 50%. This will certainly be expected to open up Ghana to the global world. This means that a lot of investment in broadband infrastructure, skills development, reduction or abolishing of taxes for CPE and PCs and stimulation of broadband by government will have to be done to achieve the above objectives. Other measures may include tax relief and broadband infrastructure development in the rural areas. These are some other factors that influence broadband penetration in Ghana.

4.2 50% Broadband Penetration by 2015

The proposed national broadband strategy seeks to achieve 10 percent penetration yearly for the next five years effective 2010. The current rate of broadband penetration is 0.3% and the idea is to increase it to 50 percent in five years. This will certainly call for some form of direct intervention from the government and some kind of collaboration with the private sector.

The Ghana government has awarded a $150 million contract to Huawei Technologies, a Chinese-based ICT and telecommunication infrastructure company, to provide modern infrastructure to ensure internet broadband availability countrywide within the next 24 month.

4.3 Anticipated Increase in GDP growth to 6.9% in the next 5 years

In terms of economic indication, it is estimated to increase Ghana's Gross Domestic Product (GDP) by 6.9 percent, and every one out of two Ghanaians is expected to have broadband access. Though it looks "over ambitious", it is possible to attain these set targets. Ghana is placed 28th of the 56 Africa countries in terms of internet access. These are some measures that government is putting in place to make broadband available to Ghanaians.

Investing in broadband is an indirect investment in economic development. It means that broadband must be made accessible and affordable to all in order to achieve the set targets discussed.

Broadband is now recognized to be a strategic priority by many developing and emerging economies, as it is seen to be a driving force in the move towards a knowledge-based economy. It is also a means to achieve social and economic benefits in areas such as health and education.

4.4 Broadband penetration and Government Requirements

In order to deliver these benefits, the broadband industry must be tailored to the country's needs.

Ministries and regulators responsible for broadband will therefore need to consider making interventions to "incentivize" extension of coverage, if this is a policy priority. The need for public and private organizations to set up portals to facilitate transactions with stakeholders should become paramount under such circumstances. This is because these portals should be designed to provide all services that stakeholders will require from any organization be it private or public. Affordability of broadband services is another area in which policy and regulation has a role to play in order to ensure competitive pricing along the supply chain from international connectivity to end-user service provision.

Creating successful broadband policies in developing countries identifies the benefits of broadband. Internet access for citizens, communities and businesses in developing countries, and describes strategies by which regulators and policymakers can help to advance these, using case studies of previously successful policy implementations.

This project identifies actions that can help to overcome some of the key challenges in stimulating widespread broadband coverage, ensuring cost-oriented pricing and making broadband valuable to the end user. These include "incentivising" private-sector investment, identifying the circumstances that drive the need for specific regulatory intervention and implementing programs in areas such as IT literacy and e-government services.

http://www.analysysmason.com/Research/Content/Reports/RRG02-Creating-successful-broadband-policies/ cited 02/02/2010 @ 5:46 am

There is the need to transform Ghana into a knowledge based society and technology driven economy. This cannot be achieved with the current level of education.

4.5 Education and ICT Skills Improvement

Education level in Ghana is relatively low and it is worse in the rural areas where illiteracy thrives. Government should address the issue of getting well educated rural settlers who will then appreciate the use of the internet as a tool for development, growth and also as a means of communicating faster and cheaper to the outside world. The potentials of the internet should be "visible" to the rural dweller.

Chapter Five

"What Strategies Should Be Put In Place To Increase Broadband Penetration In Rural Areas In Ghana?"

5.1 Approaches to Policy Design

Ghana is a developing country with broadband penetration of 0.3% and internet access penetration of 4.2%. Ghana's per capita income GDP is US$ 670.00, it implies that income levels are very low compared to Europe's US$20,000 and more. Another important factor is that the literacy rate in the rural areas is very low. It must be noted that literacy rate in Ghana is just under 60% which is dominantly urban based. With these low figures, a lot of work needs to be done to increase broadband penetration in Ghana as a whole and the rural areas in particular.

To design successful broadband policy for the rural areas in Ghana, and with the set targets in mind, this project finds it important to consider the following questions:

- What are the benefits that broadband can bring to the rural populace in Ghana?
- What are the potential barriers to a private investor and what policies can be used to overcome these barriers?
- How can a regulator reduce the risk for an investor in the broadband market?
- What are the potential bottlenecks in the supply chain that must be removed in order to reduce prices to the end user?
- How can spectrum policy be designed to encourage investment in the rural areas?
- How can the policymakers decrease the cost of broadband use to the end user?
- What can Ghana learn (broadband policy) from the experience of other countries?
- How can the "broadband gap" between urban and rural areas be addressed?
- How can government increase education and ICT skills development in the rural areas?
- How can the energy issues be addressed, especially in the rural areas?

The above questions are important for any potential designer of broadband policy for the rural areas not only in Ghana but also for developing countries as a whole. This is because the questions take into consideration the benefits of broadband to the end user in the rural areas, issues on how to cut down broadband cost, while protecting the investor who has to make huge investment in broadband infrastructure. It also takes into consideration the experiences the regulator can learn from other countries that embarked on a similar course of broadband penetration. Finally, the issue of energy to power the systems for broadband is also addressed.

5.1.1 Benefits of Broadband to the Rural Populace

Broadband penetration brings about several benefits considering the economics of it. In summary, benefits can be seen in the areas of Agriculture, Education, Industry, health, governance, communications, finance, commerce, and market information, etc.

This section (benefits of broadband to the rural populace) will be treated in detail in the next chapter.

5.1.2 Potential Barriers to Private Investor and Policies that can overcome these Barriers

In most developing countries, investors generally have a hard time registering their businesses, implementing their plans and repatriating profits. Policies should be clearly spelt out to protect the investor so as not to dampen his hopes and lose his investment. This will clearly send out wrong signals to other investors. Registration and issuing of license should not be unduly delayed especially by the regulator and the registrar of companies. Some time limit must be set, as a matter of policy, for the registration period and also for the regulator to issue out license once all underground investigation has been done about the investor and cleared to do business.

As a matter of fact, leasing or renting land on which to erect their structures such as masts and generators are in some cases fraught with litigation right from the issue of land ownership to health implication on neighbors following the erection of masts. Most lands, as a result of the inheritance system, have problems with ownership. The ideal situation would have been for telecom companies to secure government lands for their needs but unfortunately government lands are normally for government purposes and not for privates operations. Again, the location of government lands may not fit into their network design. Despite all these issues, another look at the "litigation free" government lands can be considered for companies sending broadband to the rural areas in Ghana, provided government lands fit into their network design.

It may therefore be necessary to put in place policies to protect the investor with regard to land lease for the purpose of broadband penetration in the rural areas. It should be possible for some time limit to be set for resolution of land issues that may appear before the judiciary to be treated with early dispatch in order not to kill the investment by unnecessarily delaying the outcome of judgment. As the saying goes, justice delayed is justice denied.

The political climate in most developing countries is characterized by unstable governments courtesy coup de tat. Investment and coup run parallel (ie they do not meet) and as a result no investor will like to put his money where there is an unstable government. A more stable government of democratic tendencies has the potential to woo investors. This may currently not be applicable to Ghana, but then it applies to some other developing countries.

5.1.3 How can a regulator reduce the risk for an investor in the broadband market?

Reducing the risk for an investor by the regulator may take several forms. These may include but not limited to the following;

    a. Addressing systematic or repeated risk to investors
    b. Protecting investors (and consumers)
    c. Eliminating gabs in the regulatory structure in favor of investors (and consumers)
    d. Fostering international coordination

Policies may occasionally be made to address the above factors as and when they arise. Approaching the above issues quickly is the mark of an efficient and effective regulator.

5.1.4 What are the potential bottlenecks in the supply chain that must be removed in order to reduce prices to the end user?

We can look at the supply chain as consisting of the 3 elements of bandwidth. These are international bandwidth, national bandwidth and last mile bandwidth.

International bandwidth is the upstream connectivity. It could be undersea cables, satellite or microwave. In Ghana for example, the undersea cables are SAT3 and lately GLO-1. MainONE is yet to arrive though it is expected this year (2010). There are some satellites which are also used for upstream connectivity.

National bandwidth is the platform for the transmission and distribution of international bandwidth from one point to the other within the country.

Last mile bandwidth is the delivery of national bandwidth to the end users' offices and homes. This is done by the telecoms/iSPs.

At the international bandwidth, satellites were initially used for upstream connectivity. Later, the incumbent (Ghana Telecom turned Vodafone) got undersea cable (SAT3). SAT3 was the only undersea cable that was in Ghana until recently. Though prices from SAT3 were cheaper than the expensive and inefficient satellites, Ghana Telecom still had its charges on a high side comparatively to rates in Europe as a result of the monopoly she enjoyed. The incumbent enjoyed this monopoly which was a bottleneck to the end user because they always took advantage of this (monopoly) to increase prices. Their inefficient and loss making operations were always passed on to the consumer. This bottleneck has been removed by privatizing the telecommunication sector. It is for this reason that GLO-1 just arrived in Ghana from London and MainONE is due to arrive from Portugal soon. Privatizing the telecom sector will eventually remove the monopoly enjoyed by Vodafone and be replaced with a free market where prices are expected to fall as a result of demand and supply forces at work.

Also at the national level, due to differences in distance, it is very expensive to send broadband from Accra to Tamale. For example driving an international e1 which cost $4,500 from Accra to Tamale (for example) will have an additional cost of $1,300, plus $2,500 activation fee. This results in serious disparities in pricing and as a result there is lack of broadband in such areas – "Broadband Gap". There could be the possibility of granting a tax holiday or to those who send broadband to such areas or the government providing some subsidy for this course. It is also important that more firms are introduced at the national bandwidth to forestall the possibility of popping up cartels to dictate prices.

The cost of Customer Premise Equipment and PCs are very expensive. This is largely due to the taxes that are put on them by the government. Prices range from $200 to $10,000 for these items. Policies may be put in place to remove all these taxes which will serve as a huge incentive to all Ghanaians in our bid to acquire PCs and get access to the internet. This idea will certainly stimulate broadband use once prices are moderate.

In some cases, it is not all an issue of public policy that will have to be designed to achieve a goal. For example, at the last mile bandwidth, driving bandwidth to individual homes is expensive. To cut down on cost, people within a locality can get together to bargain and negotiate with the ISP for lower prices. Also, the district assemblies can think about organizing with the ISP to get clients in bulk for lower prices.

5.1.5 How can spectrum policy be designed to encourage investment in the rural areas?

The objective of spectrum management include: rationalize and optimize the use of spectrum; avoid and solve problems of interference; design short range and long range frequency allocation, advance introduction of new wireless technology; coordinate wireless communication with neighbors and other administrations. (source: http://en.wikipedia.org/wiki/Spectrum_management) cited 09/03/2010 @ 22:00

The demand for spectrum is for services such as broadcasting, mobile, fixed, radio navigation, satellite communication and research among others.

Effective Spectrum management requires regulation at the national, regional and global levels. Because spectrum is a finite resource, its allocation requires efficient and effective coordination. In Ghana, the regulator (National Communications Authority (NCA)) is the central authority for spectrum allocation and usage decisions. The regulator issues licenses based on the services available and a business plan submitted by the investor. However, in the last year, the regulator started the auctioning of frequencies for cellular purposes which was won by GLO for the first time. Auctioning provides a more efficient way of leasing frequencies thereby stimulating competition among investors. Though the winner of the auction is assigned the spectrum, he cannot resell it. It is returned to the regulator if unused.

The justification of auctioning spectrum can be found in the light of unpredictable technology and also the demand for spectrum which cannot be determined not even by

29

the regulator. With technological development, the most efficient way of leasing frequencies is by auction which will create an environment for its efficient use.

The traditional method where government allocates spectrum rights seems to inhibit innovation and competition.

5.1.6 How can the policymakers decrease the cost of broadband use to the end user?

All the above issues raised and tackled, if well implemented, may result in reduction in the cost of broadband in the rural areas.

5.1.7 What can Ghana learn (broadband policy) from the experience of other countries?

It is obvious that there is a large store of experiences available to Ghana from the advanced, middle income (South Korea) and even the developing countries like Morocco, Tunisia, Egypt, etc. It is a matter of under studying these experiences and tailoring their policies to suit the Ghana terrain. It means that we could pick lessons from advanced, middle income and developing economies. Though we could pick some lessons from a country like South Korea, their urban planning is different from Ghana's. A lot can also be learnt from other developing and developed countries like the e-Europe approach. Ghana should however be careful not to just take any whole sale "treatment". This is because some policies may not fit into our set up.

5.1.8 How can the "broadband gap" between urban and rural areas be addressed?

"Broadband gap" is the geographical differences in broadband access, speed, quality of service (QoS), pricing and use between urban and rural/remote areas.

This issue can be solved through some technological and pricing innovation.

Government, as a matter of policy, may introduce fixed wireless and WiFi technologies in the various districts or remote areas. Also, there is the need for government to somehow play a "Robin Hood" by taxing urban customers to subsidize rural use of broadband.

Rural areas are normally sparsely populated and also usage is not as heavy as it is in the urban areas. This solution may encourage migration to the rural areas thus reversing the rural urban migration.

5.1.9 How can government increase education and ICT skills development in the rural areas?

The approach here is simply to look for money, put into the national budget for the above purpose. Since it is assumed that broadband penetration will bring about the expected growth in the country, and especially higher growth in the rural areas, it is imperative for

the government to do the expected economic analysis, compared to other sectors and if the figures are encouraging, then money may be voted for this purpose.

Based on some of the suggestions made earlier, government can bring in investors to build broadband infrastructure in the rural areas. It can also team up with some investors for this purpose. The government may also build such infrastructure for the rural folks.

5.1.10 How can energy issues be addressed especially in the rural areas?

This question may be easy to digest but difficult to implement. Of the 22 million or more Ghanaians, as many as 9 million do not access to electricity. Those without power are mainly based in the rural areas. This is a serious challenge to policy makers because without energy, all the above strategies will not provide us with the expected results. There cannot be 50% access to broadband nationwide when the energy sector is not responsive to the needs of broadband infrastructure. The 6.9% growth in GDP will only be a mirage should energy issues remain unresolved.

In the light of it, the project recommends the following;

a. Government must explore and find ways of building more hydro dams for power generation. In fact, hydro is a much cheaper source of power generation than thermal which is the next option.

b. In case generating power by hydro alone cannot meet the energy requirements of the country, we can complement it by thermal power generation to boost the energy production in the country.

c. Generators are the other option to be considered, but it involves lot of capital. In the case of Ghana, the government is building another dam at Bui in the Brong Ahafo region to complement the Akosombo hydro electric dam. In addition to the Akosombo hydro power generation plant, there is a thermal plant at Abandzie in the Western Region of Ghana which contributes to power production in Ghana.

There are other private power developers and lots of generators being used nationwide in offices and in our homes. However, lots more power is needed to power the rural areas as well as some parts of the urban areas as well.

Other options like solar and wind power which are not very popular can be explored to complement the others specified.

5.2 Strategies to Increase Broadband Penetration in Rural Areas in Ghana

Based on the above issues raised and analyzed, to achieve the aim of this project, any public policy designed for increased broadband penetration in the rural areas in Ghana (and possibly other developing countries) can take some or all the following strategies into consideration. These are:

a. The need to liberalize the telecommunication market to encourage competition and break the monopoly of the incumbent.

b. The need to protect the investor from the time of registering to do business in Ghana to repatriation of profits

c. Protect end user in the rural areas by streamlining supply chain and breaking all other possible monopoly not only at the international bandwidth but at the national bandwidth and also last mile bandwidth. This can be done by policy to introduce competition at all levels of the supply chain

d. Subsidy can be granted the rural populace for broadband use and charging "higher" for urban use (if possible) – "Robin Hood" style

e. Abolish taxes (if need be) on broadband infrastructure, built in the rural areas.

f. Government may also consider abolishing taxes on all PCs arriving in Ghana to boost their use.

g. Possible tax holiday for investors who build broadband infrastructure in the rural areas in Ghana.

h. Policy that will overcome potential barriers to an investor as it occurs because values of society is not static

i. Policy to protect end user by way of Quality of Service (QoS)

j. Policy to encourage government private partnership in investing in broadband infrastructure

k. The need to develop policy to encourage skills development in the rural areas

l. Policy to increase computer literacy levels in the rural areas

m. Policy to invest some percentage of talk tax (communication tax) in broadband infrastructure development in the rural areas

n. The need to increase broadband bandwidth from 256kbps to 2Mbps

o. Policy to address energy needs of the rural areas and Ghana as a whole. 9,000,000 Ghanaians mostly in the rural areas do not have access to electricity. (ref "The Daily Graphic" 27th February 2010 edition Page …)

Apart from public policy as a strategy to increase broadband penetration in the rural areas, there are other ways to do that. These include;

a. Arrangements between rural authorities and ISPs
b. Companies operating in the rural areas and ISPs
c. Educational institutions (tertiary in particular)
d. Industries (eg mining companies) implementing broadband in the rural areas

These are individual/organizational initiatives (private policy) to provide broadband to their organizations in the rural areas.

As a matter of fact these initiatives are what have provided broadband to the rural areas as at now, though negligible in percentage terms.

In view of the above points to be considered as strategies (policy) for broadband penetration in the rural areas, it is imperative to discuss the benefits of broadband penetration to the populace in the rural areas in Ghana.

Chapter Six

Expected Benefits of Broadband Penetration in Rural Ghana

6.1 Benefits

The previous chapters threw light on strategies as public policy to encourage broadband penetration in the rural areas in Ghana. This chapter will concentrate on the benefits that broadband penetration will bring to the rural populace in Ghana assuming it is well implemented.

The project will examine these benefits in the areas of Agriculture, Education, Industry, health, governance, communications, finance, commerce, and market information. It is expected that policies well implemented can transform positively the living standards of the rural population in Ghana.

6.2 Agriculture (e-Agriculture)

Ghana is an Agriculture based economy. It is a producer of primary products. Over 60% of her workforce is in the Agric sector. It is unfortunate that despite this huge workforce in this sector, output is on subsistence scale. It means that output from this sector is generally low. Farmers who produce the bulk of the produce are mostly illiterates and are aging. This gives cause for concern since the future for this sector does not look bright. Agriculture extension officers who are to educate the farmers are themselves not up to date with modern technology such as the use of computers and the internet, and even in their own Agric profession. Their knowledge is somehow limited in training the farmers. They are supposed to be the backbone of the farmers to increase their farms and yields.

The introduction of broadband in the rural areas, coupled with educating the Extension officers and farmers on the use and benefits of computers and the internet will therefore do a lot to boost production. The extension officer will be expected to acquire more knowledge by using the internet. They can communicate conveniently with the farmers via email or portal for the farmers to access. They could also exchange ideas with their foreign counterparts to share experiences and knowledge. The educated and informed farmers can also access the internet to upgrade themselves with advanced farming methods. They can on their own study to know other crops suitable for the soil on which they farm. They can also introduce new products to increase output. They may also acquire knowledge in increasing their yield per acre courtesy the internet. Through the use of the internet, they may have access to new farming tools and accessories.

Farmers may communicate among themselves to share ideas and also with other farmers abroad about current trends in farming and potential markets for their produce. This can result in joint ventures between Ghanaian farmers and those in the developed world with their sophisticated machinery to increase production in Ghana.

The market queens who purchase the produce of these farmers get them at very cheap prices. This is because the farmers have no where else to turn to for better prices for their produce. This has kept the farmers in abject poverty. The introduction of the internet means that they can stay on their farms and scout for better prices on the internet. They can be in a better position to possibly get foreign markets for better prices for their products. A side advantage to the farmers also is that their children can access the internet to educate themselves for better education and exposure.

6.3 Education (e-Education)

In the field of education, the internet can play a very significant role in the rural settings of Ghana. The internet abounds with enough knowledge. Most parts of the rural areas in Ghana are without enough qualified teachers. This means that people with very limited educational backgrounds take up the mantle as teachers. These "teachers" are termed "Pupil teachers". The "pupil teachers" may take advantage of the presence of broadband to learn from the internet to add value to their teaching. In some cases, they may be taught to provide support for systems in the rural settings.

With enough understanding of the internet and broadband introduced in an environment, teachers, students and pupils may take advantage of this to do their studies and possibly get more than what they may be taught at school. The application of Video on Demand (VOD) may be used in this case. It means already stored programs (in this case educational programs), to the levels of the student/pupils may be accessed for knowledge.

The government in its bid to solve the teaching problems in these areas can get the syllabi of the various classes and forms taught and stored in a library. The library can be accessed by the various rural pupils where teachers are not available to teach. This will go a long way to solve the problem of lack of teachers in the rural areas. Occasionally or programmed, there could also be live presentations on the internet. Students can then access these presentations and ask question during live presentations, courtesy video conference. Though certain people may see it as impossible for now, it may even be cheaper to get one good and qualified teacher making a presentation nationwide to all pupils who access the service on government bill than getting and paying thousands of teachers all over the rural settings. This is food for thought.

The internet may offer children in the rural areas a lot of exposure in their lifestyle. Like a knife, there may be good and bad sides to the internet. Students and pupils should then be guided when accessing the internet.

Education is not limited to only the young students and pupils, but also to adults who may not have been privileged to get education in their youth. They may be introduced to education during the non-formal education programs and have access to the internet which is a wealth of knowledge.

6.4 Industry (e-Industry)

Most industries in Ghana are urban based. Broadband has the potential of moving industries to the rural areas. This is because with most of the raw materials being rural based and very high taxes imposed on industries located in the cities, broadband can ensure communications within and outside the firm, even in rural areas. It must be noted that communication systems within the rural areas is nothing to write home about. It means that more firms may choose to relocate where the potential raw material is based and pay lower taxes with good communication networks. It also means that cost of moving raw materials from the source to the factory may reduce significantly as the rural areas may be seen as the source of raw materials, though not in all cases.

This also means creating jobs for the rural folks. The rural folks may be employed by some of these industries. The effect will be a reduction in the rural-urban migration which has over burdened the cities and been a nightmare to the government. Provided there is guaranteed employment in the rural areas, there will be very little justification for moving to the urban centers for jobs. Setting up industries in the rural areas is a sure way of boosting these areas and raising their standard of living.

6.5 Health (e-Health)

Health is a very important aspect in our lives as it cuts across urban and rural settings. Generally, the urban areas are better endowed with medical facilities than the rural areas. They have the best medical personnel, teaching hospitals, pharmacy, laboratories, and top class private hospitals, etc.

The rural areas are generally not well endowed in terms of medics, hospitals, clinics, pharmacy, etc. In most cases, they have small medical centers which are manned by doctors who may not be specialists or Administrators as compared to the urban hospitals manned by Hospital Administrators, Specialists and other professionals.

In extreme medical cases in the rural areas, patients are normally referred to the bigger health centers in the urban centers for treatment due to lack of know how or facilities in the rural areas. Some of these problems can be solved when broadband bandwidth is available in the rural areas.

Introducing broadband bandwidth in the rural areas means knowledge triumphing over illiteracy, ignorance and superstition. These are as a result of lack of education. In our rural areas, illiteracy is serious to the extent that diseases like malaria fever, HIV AIDS, CSM and others are attributed to superstition. Once education is increased with the use of computer and the internet, ignorance and illiteracy will give way to knowledge, scientific analysis and truth. The rural folks will themselves now obtain knowledge of symptoms they experience and get better understanding of issues affecting their health.

With the advent of video conferencing, general practitioners in the rural settings can make very good use of their more experienced specialists to conduct operations in the

theatres of the rural health centers. It means that long travels by the specialists to the rural areas to treat patients will be cut down considerably. Another advantage of video conferencing to the health sector is that with guidance of specialists, there will be very minimal referral cases from the rural to urban hospitals. The rural doctor may also gain knowledge from the internet to gain more knowledge and increase the quality of service that he delivers to the rural areas. Nurses and technologists/technicians in the rural areas stand the chance of gaining knowledge from the world wide net to increase on their services.

Chat facility can help the rural doctor consult the more experienced urban doctors on the spot when treating a patient and seeks advice. Exchange of ideas will now come in conveniently.

Pharmacists could take advantage of a chat site to communicate with other colleagues about their stock levels especially when drugs needed in the hospital are in short supply in the rural areas but in abundant else where. The technicians can do same for their equipment and study new and better ways of diagnosing patients for their ailments.

Occasionally, the various professional bodies in the health sector may take advantage of video conferencing facilities to educate members about new discoveries in their areas courtesy broadband which enables data convergence with ease.

Health professionals in the rural areas can take advantage of SKPE, Facebook, etc to communicate among themselves.

6.6 Governance (e-Governance)

E-Governance is the public sector's use of information and communication technologies with the aim of improving information and service delivery, encouraging citizen participation in the decision-making process and making government more accountable, transparent and effective.

(source: http://portal.unesco.org/ci/en/ev.php-URL_ID=3038&URL_DO=DO_TOPIC&URL_SECTION=201.html cited 27/02/2010 @ 06:21 am)

People in the rural areas may take advantage of the internet to make suggestions and express their views on government decisions, policies and laws of the land..

ICT could be used to enhance good governance. By this tool, government is expected to be more accountable to the citizens of the land.

Their knowledge and views on the constitutions can be expressed on various sites for government officials to consider these views when developing policies or drafting laws. This will prompt government to take into consideration views from the general public.

37

Issues of human rights can be seen from the rural perspective and horrible stories on human rights abuses will be quickly exposed. Government officials in the rural areas will be more responsive to their problems and not lord it over them as it is in some cases.

Their views on the legislature and decisions on judgments in our courts will go a long way to consolidate democracy in the rural areas and also the country as a whole.

Views expressed will influence not only government policy but also electoral decisions both in their localities and nationwide elections.

Various political groups in the rural areas can take advantage of networking sites like Facebook and others to communicate among themselves when at home and other places.

6.7 Finance (e-Finance)

E-Finance is about fund management. It is about business, public finance and private finance.

In the rural areas, there are lots of small scale enterprises that can take advantage of broadband bandwidth to expand their businesses via the internet.

Previously, financial houses such as the banks, insurance companies, etc found it difficult to monitor and give loans to small scale enterprises. This was because monitoring such clients was not easy and especially when they did not have any valued collateral. With the advent of broadband in rural areas, the banks and other financial institutions can take advantage of it to monitor clients via mobile phones and internet use. Potential clients can also be roped into main stream banking courtesy mobile banking that can help access banking and insurance services.

Other small scale money lenders and collectors will take advantage of the broadband penetration to also advertise their products and create portal to enable their clients access their contributions or occasionally text them their statements or balances.

6.8 Commerce (e-Commerce)

This is that art of trading in goods and services on the internet. There are so many sites that rural businessmen can take advantage of to join as members, advertise and sell their products. By advertising on the internet, the globe is the limit of the advert. The buyer in Norway can purchase sweet pepper from a trader in the rural Ghana possibly at a higher price and bigger volumes compared to the market queens who dictate prices to them and leave them in abject poverty.

Market information also helps in this area because buyers and sellers will have access to competitive prices of what they want to trade or buy. This will help them fix competitive prices for their product or bargain for good prices.

6.9 Communications (e-Communications)

This business of internet and broadband is about communications. Members of the rural community can communicate among themselves and outside the rural setting when broadband infrastructure is in place. With the advent of broadband, convergence of voice, video and data makes it possible to see and communicate with somebody from afar conveniently as you see and talk to that person eg. SKYPE.

There are chat rooms that you can communicate through video, voice and data (text).

There are also content providers who develop services. These services may be available to the rural folks to make live more convenient than it is without broadband infrastructure..

For example, the rural folks may experience the convenience of sitting in the comfort of their homes and transferring money from their bank accounts to pay their children's fees or transfer money to settle domestic bills like water and electricity bills. They may no longer make trips to go and post application letters but will stay at home and fill job vacancies via the internet and email their CVs for job vacancies. They may communicate with their relatives and love ones abroad from their homes as they see every action of the relative or loved ones.

They can talk to business partners, search for businesses and markets, check, on market information to do business and many more. Students can take advantage of the internet for live presentations by lecturers from afar, access libraries courtesy Video on Demand (VOD).

The earlier points that were raised in this chapter all fall under the category of e-communications. In short, e-Communication is the umbrella of the benefits raised.

·

Chapter Seven

Conclusion

7.1 Project Expectations

It is the expectation of this project that drawing up public policy for broadband penetration for the rural areas in Ghana will consider the issues raised in the preceding chapters. They are relevant in policy drawing because all possible issues that have to do with investors, end users, ISPs and regulators have been properly discussed. It must also be noted that for anyone drawing policy, there need not always be consistency in them because values of society keep changing (not static). In fact, this is what policy designers should first bear in mind.

These guidelines when properly exhausted would certainly come up with a very good policy design to fit the Ghana environment.

It must also be noted that drawing policies for broadband penetration in the rural areas of Ghana cannot be done in isolation since it will be incorporated into the national policy for broadband penetration.

At the end of the day, implementing the policy to the full and commitment of all parties to the policy designed is what matters. For example assuming there is the need to invest in broadband infrastructure and which (by an agreement) is the government's responsibility, then it must find money for it. Otherwise the concept of 50% broadband connectivity will be a mirage.

7.2 Long term Strategy

As indicated earlier, the values of society keep changing. The project for example recommended possible price subsidy for the rural users of broadband as a possible way to reverse rural urban migration. Assuming in the long term of 5 years or more, these objectives are met and the standard of living in the rural areas increase considerably as in the urban areas, then there may be the need to increase prices for rural users of broadband. This is because it can be assumed that the per capita GDP in the rural areas may have increased due to broadband penetration and other associated factors of its use in the rural/remote areas.

REFERENCE:

Adoption of Broadband Services: The role of national policies by Morten Falch

Africa Review Magazine July 2009 edition

A National Broadband strategy for economic growth and development – Draft

http://en.wikipedia.org/wiki/Africa#Territories_and_regions

http://en.wikipedia.org/wiki/Broadband_Internet_access

http://en.wikipedia.org/wiki/Spectrum_management

http://portal.unesco.org/ci/en/ev.php-URL_ID=3038&URL_DO=DO_TOPIC&URL_SECTION=201.html

http://www.afdb.org/en/news-events/article/afdb-supports-submarine-fiber-optic-cable-for-western-africa-4710/

http://www.analysysmason.com/Research/Content/Reports/RRG02-Creating-successful-broadband-policies/

http://www.internetworldstats.com/stats1.htm

http://www.nytimes.com/2009/08/10/technology/10cable.html?_r=1

http://www.websiteoptimization.com/bw/0609/european-broadband-penetration-b.gif

www.ingramcontent.com/pod-product-compliance
Lightning Source LLC
LaVergne TN
LVHW092344060326
832902LV00008B/788